Dementia Diary

POEMS & PROSE

John Killick

Published by the
Journal of Dementia Care

First published in 2008 by
Hawker Publications Ltd
Culvert House
Culvert Road
London SW11 5DH
Tel 020 7720 2108, fax 020 7498 3023

British Library Cataloguing in Publication Data

A Catalogue in Publication Data

ISBN 978 1 874 79087 7

Designed by Andrew Chapman (www.awrc.info)
Printed and bound by DG3 Europe, London

The Journal of Dementia Care is published six times a year by Hawker
Publications. For further information please contact Hawker Publications
(address above).

Other books by John Killick published by Hawker Publications:

You are words (dementia poems) Edited and introduced by John Killick
(ISBN 978 1 874 79090 7)
Openings (dementia poems and photographs) John Killick
& Carl Cordonnier (ISBN 1-874790-49-3)
Dementia Poems (audio CD) Readings exploring the experience of
memory loss, from *You are Words* and *Openings*
John Killick (ISBN 1-874790-76-6)

CONTENTS

FOREWORD

Once again John Killick reveals the inner world of people with dementia. What is so remarkable about these poems and stories is not how they take us in to worlds that are difficult to understand but in their accessibility and ordinariness. In this way these poems and stories serve to highlight the extent and depth of our shared humanity with people with dementia.

John Killick has a long standing commitment to, and track record in, capturing the essence of the experience of living with dementia. This collection is no exception. As always we are invited inside the quiet and private lives of people whom as a society we have deemed to be having no worthwhile experience. What is new in this collection is that we are brought in to the private world of the meeting between the person with dementia and the poet. We share their intimacy; feel the tenderness of their connection and their vulnerability in the face of loss.

In these poems Killick celebrates the here and now of living with dementia and maintains a respectful tone towards the joys and pains of this experience. In so doing, as in all great communication and art, the person's humour and pain becomes our own.

Killick has an uncanny ability to serve as a conduit for, and voice of, people with dementia. As always we see so much more in people with dementia through his eyes. He has a way of opening our minds, our eyes, our ears and our hearts.

For those new to Killick's work and those who eagerly await each new publication this collection is a treat. It is a privilege and a pleasure to read.

MURNA DOWNS

INTRODUCTION

I have been making poems out of the words of people with dementia for the past 15 years. My purpose in publishing them is the same as that of one of their authors: "Anything you can tell people about how things are for me is important," she said. But I don't think the best of these poems need any special pleading from me. I believe they are real poems in their raw honesty and linguistic inventiveness.

And the idea that poems made by people with dementia occupy an enclave of interest only to those with a concern for mental health and community care must be dismissed at the outset. Dementia is the ultimate existential condition, where the individual is brought up against the fundamental philosophical questions in the most stark manner possible: *Who am I? What makes for a person? How necessary is memory for identity?* And who better to provide insights into these matters than the very persons going through the process of meeting these challenges head on?

I should explain the process of the poems' composition, as it is unusual. I write down or tape-record then transcribe a person's speech. The subsequent work consists of selection, but I never alter a word. The finished poem is presented to the individual for approval and permission to publish. Though I obviously cannot completely exclude myself, my taste and proccupations as a writer, from the compilation of these texts, the aim is to let the persons speak for themselves. All the poems in Part Two of this book were created in this way.

In Part One of the book I concentrate on my own reactions, not just to the process but to the wider subject of communication. These pieces, in prose and verse, are fundamentally in my own voice, though others, including people with dementia, are quoted in them. In Part One of the sequence 'Dementia Diary' the two voices are people overheard by me.

In the final pieces in this section I tackle the ultimate mystery posed by this work: how to interact with those with more profound difficulties, including loss of speech. In 'Getting Through' the first sequence is in the imagined voice of a person with whom I am attempting to communicate; the second is what I am thinking but not speaking aloud.

I dedicate this book to all those persons whose lives have touched mine so profoundly.

JOHN KILLICK

NOTE

Some of the poetry and prose in this book has previously been published in *The London Magazine*, *Pennine Platform*, *The Journal of Dementia Care* (Hawker Publications) and its *Creativity in Dementia Care* calendars.

Some of the poems in Part Two have been broadcast on BBC Radios 3, 4 and the World Service. The last four poems are by Ian McQueen, and of these 'Taking Care of the Halo' formed the centrepiece of the programme *Still Here*, first broadcast on BBC Radio 4 in 2005.

I am most grateful to Ray Maloney, his wife Jan, and Lorraine Kremer of Michigan Alzheimer's Association for allowing me to reproduce Ray's collage 'Safe Haven' on the cover of this book. For a biography of Ray Maloney and further examples of his work see: http://optimaldementiacare.com/gallery.html

part
one

DEMENTIA DIARY

1. TWO VIEWS

They are housewives
of a tiny patch of table.
They keep polishing and polishing
and can't understand
why it never comes clean.

> *They can still take a pride*
> *in the door-panel they think they're buffing*
> *and I think they're smearing.*
> *And what's so purposeful about bingo?*

It's an underwater life
and they are the fishes.
For us at the surface
the bubbles which rise
are empty of meaning.

> *You think they're fish*
> *while we swim on the surface*
> *but they can still breathe the fresh air*
> *of human warmth.*
> *They can still give a look that kills.*

Theirs is the hardest school.
They are set to work
to unlearn everything
they have ever known.
It is no consolation
that in this task
total success is assured.

Their task to unlearn.
But they soon get to know
who they don't like,
who patronise, who don't listen,
and the ones who fob off
(no use asking her!);
not one of them can't tell
who's staff, who's fellow-resident.
And they still know how to wink!

2. TRIVIAL PURSUITS

"What is the longest insect in the world?"
Silence. Ah, a question this
of tremendous import to those for whom hobbling
to the loo seems like a journey to the end of the earth.
"Answer: it is the stick insect. It comes from Borneo."

"Now, how many arms has an octopus?"
Silence. Ah, a question this
truly to exercise the minds of those whose fingers
obstinately refuse to raise a cup of tea.
"Answer: eight. It carries out multiple tasks at once."

"Lastly, whose last words were 'Kiss me, Hardy'?"
Silence. Ah, a question this
of supreme significance to those whose minds
can barely shape the concept "Who am I?"
But whose lips will kiss and kiss and kiss...

3. MAKING CONTACT

How is it that Tom,
this Day Centre's most resolute
master of the monosyllabic negative,
keeps on smiling and smiling
and talking to me, so that
when I leave he stands in the doorway
waving and calling "Goodbye, John!
Goodbye, John!" over and over
until I am out of sight, and maybe
even after, saying "Goodbye, John!
Goodbye, John!" in his mind?

4. SEARCHING FOR SAMMY

"I'm out of husband just now.
Where is he? Have you seen him?
I'm Carrie, Carrie, carrying
a hospital bell that rings
so you wouldn't mind, would you,
if I scoured round for him?"

Off she goes, a diminutive
question-mark, opening
doors to a sluice, a store,
her pale face furrowed
by tears streaming down.

And here Sammy comes – wheeled in
from the land of broken limbs.
He calls, enfolds her in his
familiar arms, and whispers
dear somethings to reassure.

But she can't stay, she's away
again, battering at doors
with questions, calling his name.
Till, collapsed on a chair:
"I think perhaps if I sit
I might disappear a bit."

5. FRAYING

Doris pulls, pulls
at her jumper, scratches
at her skirt. She carries

a bag full of make-up, a small
clock, a teddy, a skein of wool
that's wasting from the needles.

"Home," she keeps saying,
"Home," in a flat voice.
Her eyes move everywhere.

I fear for her, fear
the garment fraying before me
won't hold together much longer.

6. GIFTS

"You do writing with these people, you say?
But they're all dementing. They've lost their way."

The door opens. Enter Meg with a vase.
Comes towards me: stagger... pause... stagger... pause...
Thrusts it out without uttering a word.
I see waxy blooms as faintly absurd.

But then the message taped to the base:
"I LOVE YOU" is what it says. And her face.

TURN OUT THE STARS

In the photograph we are standing in the unit, my left hand clasping yours. I, being much taller, am leaning forward, our heads are almost touching. We are laughing; your eyes are closed, with the intensity of the feeling, it seems. It is a shared joke, but since you have little language left it may be something we have seen and identified. Or it may be that one of us has thought of something and the merriment has spilled over onto the other. As always there is a complicity that goes beyond words.

Bodies play a big part in our relationship: we hold and hug and kiss. We are always on the move – dancing or walking – exploring our environment. You never seem to tire of new places and faces; or rather the old places and faces seem to you ever-new.

Photographs are amongst your favourite things. Your face mirrors the feelings they evoke in you, and you keep up an appropriate commentary. I can tell that by the tone of your sounds. Your discourse is full of exclamations.

Your gestures are full of exclamations: when I come on the unit and you see me in the distance you approach, always pointing, pointing.

And I do the same. Until our hands meet and intertwine. You keep saying "Oh you!" over and over, as if you cannot believe your good fortune. I cannot believe mine.

You talk to mirrors. I creep up behind to try to find out whose image you are conversing with; each time you catch sight of me and turn round. But once I manage to get close enough to hear your sister's name.

When you have a birthday celebration with your daughter and her husband you refuse to sit down at the table until I join you to help you blow out the candles on your cake. Writing this I realise I hardly know anything about your past life. What we have is all in the here-and-now. It is enough.

✳

Then last week I met one of the staff from your home and heard that you had died. I cried for quite a while. How could you go without a goodbye? I have never felt a closeness where words mattered less, so taking our leave of each other would have been a cuddling matter. I entertain a fancy where I would withdraw from you pointing all the while until you were out of sight. "Oh you, Mary!" – it seems our kind of game.

But maybe at the end it might have been no more than a shared twinkle of the eye; I refuse to believe there would have been no recognition from you of what we meant to each other, no transmitted spark.

One night I took you out into the courtyard to look at the stars. You wondered and pointed and exclaimed. You were as grateful as if I had turned them on personally. Now the stars are turned out for you. One star, too, is dimmed for me.

DEMENTIA HAIKU

Lucky lady said
"Problems with my memory?
Well, I've forgotten."

"Everyone here
has Alzheimer's except me
and no one else knows."

This gift I bring you,
please handle it carefully:
it is the present.

LOCKED IN

Margaret brings Susan through from the main room of the day centre to meet me. She is walking slowly, unsteadily, and looking from side to side. She is short, thin, slightly bowed, and seems much in need of support. She is smartly dressed, with shiny black shoes, a pale lemony blouse, and a long elegant black coat. Around her neck is a new multicoloured silk scarf. The contrast with her face is marked. It is very pale but she wears no make-up. Her cheeks are sunken in, and there are worry-lines everywhere. Her eyes are pale, rheumy and scared-looking. Her hair is silvery and thinning. I guess she might be in her early eighties.

She sighs frequently, and squirms on her chair in front of me. Occasionally she brushes or picks at her coat removing hairs or stains real or imaginary. Many of her sentences end with the word 'love', which is both endearing and suggestive of a degree of subservience.

Her voice is rather faint and her tones are anxiety-laden. In between contributions she gazes into the distance, but not for long, always withdrawing from her reverie with intimations of a new aspect of her life which is causing her concern. She shows us a tiny oval picture of a bearded holy man she keeps tightly clutched in her palm. "He has the stigmata," she explains. "I can't go to Mass any more. He works for me sometimes."

Susan speaks of the accident which had occurred three years before. She had slipped on some ice outside her house and broken her hip. This had necessitated a stay of some weeks in hospital, and she had returned home disoriented and fearful. Her husband was already disabled and in a wheelchair and she found she could no longer look after him, so their daughter, who lived not far away, had taken him in. She had lived alone since then, which offered maximum opportunity for things to prey on her mind.

On the other hand she values her independence. She still cooks for herself, but a home help comes in and does her housework. Susan burned herself making the toast a few days previously and shows us the scar on the back of her hand.

The doctor is treating her for depression, and she takes her medication regularly. However, she is unable to find peace of mind. The thoughts that keep flooding in make her extremely agitated. A therapist at the centre has lent her a relaxation tape which she listens to regularly.

"Do you find it helpful?" asks Margaret. "Yes. Well that's what I tell her so as not to upset her," says Susan.

Throughout the conversation we gain a vivid picture of what it must be like to be continually beset by doubts and presagings of the end of it all. Susan says:

> "It's all in here when I get up in the morning. It's in here when I go to bed at night. It's all in my head and I can't get away from it. I walk up and down all the time in my house and I can't get away from it."

She used to watch the television but now she can't put it on for fear of the characters and the words they utter entering a consciousness which is already overburdened. As it is, names will keep coming into her mind:

> "If there's a name mentioned I have to write it down. I write all the names down. I don't know what to do with them, but I have to write them down. I have notebooks full of them."

Susan hasn't ventured outside the house on her own since the accident: "I open the front door and I think I'm going to fall." She has, however, kept coming to the day centre, but each time she says: "I shouldn't have come. I think this visit will be my last." She gave herself a scare a day or two after injuring her hand on the toaster: "I got up the other morning and I saw spots of blood on my nightie. I thought I was going to die."

I get the strong impression that there is little anyone can do for Susan any more. Just as she is self-imprisoned in her house, she is closeted with the terrors in her skull. This diminutive figure in black is a walking embodiment of nightmare; she seems possessed by a particularly potent kind of death-wish. I could take her in my arms and attempt to console her but to no avail:

> "I'll never get any better, love. It's an awful thing, fear. I've got it inside of me, and I know I'll never be rid of it now."

APPROACHING THE MYSTERY

She lies in a wide armchair, back to the window, with the sun streaming through the glass. It is being used as a kind of bed; she is supported by pillows, with her body wrapped in a blanket, and a teddy bear laid to one side. She appears very old, and her face is hollowed, lined and pale. Her hair is white, thinly layered and straggles down her cheeks. The glasses perched on her nose seem like an afterthought. The lounge of the nursing home is hers alone, apart from my presence as a visitor. The room is without sound. One can only tell that she is alive by the measured rise and fall of her chest. This, one feels, is what her life essentially has come to: the steady intake and exhalation, a pulse, a heartbeat – the mechanics of existence.

How could it be otherwise? Probably speech has gone, and medication makes sleep the only option. Age and infirmity have taken their toll. Choices have been winnowed to this last alternative – to breathe or not to breathe. Which is no choice at all, since she is unlikely any longer to have the capacity to exercise it.

So how much of the human remains? Is what I observe the last unwindings of a spring set in motion by her conception, wholly pre-dictable in its trajectory? Or does she still dream? If dreaming requires the experience of everyday to feed it, then maybe the stream of uncon-scious processing during sleep has dried up. Or are her fantasies still succoured by a lifetime's memories? The body's dissolution may have robbed her of mobility, and her mind's capacity to observe and process in a conventional way, but ninety years of bombardment of the senses, engagement of the emotions, and interpretation of reality must surely still be there, miraculously preserved, and may still be accessible.

In the recording lock of her brain she will carry the imprint of almost a century of turbulent social change, the most dramatic experienced by any generation in history. Not only have their lives been incomparably eventful in outward terms but they have been longer in duration than those of their forebears, giving them a greater bank of memories upon which to draw.

Looking at this woman before me I am led to speculate on her life – what events have shaped her, has she experienced the highs and lows of existence, or has she maintained an equilibrium, living largely uneventfully and untroubled? Has her frame been stirred with passion, and the barely supportable knowledge of its being returned? Or have her days been informed by a steady and constant affection, to lull her into the illusion of permanence? Does this love still sustain her in her present removed state?

Maybe there is someone even now who cherishes her and comes here regularly to sit and watch over her for signs of recognition. If so, I wonder if she would be aware of their comings and goings. It might be a comfort to her, or is she past caring? On the other hand, the pain of this situation might be too much for the other person to bear. Is any life worth the selfless devotion that would be necessary to sustain this commitment? And yet if relationship is to mean anything then surely this is just the circumstance which provides the testing-ground – the greatest need existing where no need is manifest?

And then there is the environment in which this last scene is being played out. It is not a place she is likely to have chosen. The surroundings are impersonal. Those charged with caring for her are strangers fulfilling a role. Is love to be demanded of them, and, if so, how is it to be supplied? Surely they seek a sign, however fleeting, that their presence is acknowledged. This could be anybody (any body) before them. There may be no biography to go on, and insufficient evidence of their senses to supply the lack. They will only have a generalised concept of the human to fall back on. It is a challenge which cannot be refused, but how is it to be met?

Then again, does this woman actually have dementia? Because of greater longevity she belongs to a generation in which there has been a greater prevalence of the condition than ever before, so the likelihood of her having developed it is substantial. Dementia can send a cloudy glass almost opaque. To the effects of her physical frailty, and the drugs that may have been prescribed to alleviate it, may have to be added communication problems consequent on her dementia. We are only at the beginning of trying to find out the effects of this upon the person. Perhaps in some people this leads to a lack of awareness which, though it inhibits our attempts to get close to them, may shield them from the knowledge of what is happening to them. It may be, of course, that some individuals experience dementia as a waking nightmare from which sleep offers them little relief. It could be possible that the condition in some obscure way prepares people for the inevitable when it occurs. Whatever the cause the effect may present itself as a process of withdrawal.

But there are other possible causes of withdrawal. Suppose this woman is withdrawn because others have withdrawn from her? Her present isolation would then be a response rather than an inevitable consequence of her condition. Other people may be responsible for what I observe in her; she could be fulfilling a role, playing out their desires. If she has been offered no chance of relationship then there is a sense in which her mind has been condemned to death in the same way as disease or age have condemned her body. Even if I could establish that what I am witnessing is withdrawal I have no way of knowing the cause or causes of that state.

Nor, if what I am witnessing is withdrawal, have I any way of knowing the intensity or otherwise of her inwardness. Whether the withdrawal goes further, involves perhaps a reaching out towards a state which succeeds this, is also something about which I can only speculate.

The ends of our existence dissolve into pure mystery. And would we have it otherwise? It lends a sense of challenge and excitement to our lives. Without travelling out from and towards the unknown we might be tempted to lapse into the kind of mindless habituation which can beset our middle years. It keep us on our toes intellectually, sharpens our spiritual reflexes. Why were we given consciousness of self if not to ponder the dissolution or enhancement of the spirit? Mystics and other contemplatives may have leaned too far in the other direction and neglected the body's demands, but they perhaps win out in being more prepared for what may follow.

Throughout my reflections the woman on the chair in front of me does not appear to have moved. She has vouchsafed no clue as to her awareness or otherwise of her situation. She remains half in bed, half out of it; perhaps half in life, half out of it? My empathy goes out to her in her profound isolation. My hand goes out to her in reassurance... do I imagine a slight pressure of hers in response?

REASONS

"Why do you keep chipping away at that huge piece of rock?"
the little boy asked Michelangelo. "Because I know
there's an angel inside trying to get out."

"Why do I keep gazing at, stroking, whispering to
this body in a bed?" I ask myself. "Because I know
there's a person inside trying to get out."

GETTING THROUGH (1)

1

I open my mouth
and I close it again
on silence. Nothing comes out.
Like a fish out of water –
words were my element.
With some it's moaning.
With some it's drivel.
With some it's dribble.
With me it's keeping my peace
because I have no choice.
I take it all in
but I give nothing back.
Nobody knows how I feel.
Nobody knows what I want.
Nobody knows ME.

2

A door slamming over
and over. Each time it bangs
It wakes me or makes me jump.
Doors are for passing through –
I never go anywhere. I know
nothing of what lies
on the other side. Only the
incessant door-banging
to remind me of movement,
passage, destinations,
elsewheres I shall never see.
Please take that door away!

3

Is anyone there?
I listen for voices, words
I can recognise and respond to.
But all I can hear is shouts,
screams, orders, snatches
of conversations, occasional laughs.
They are all there: the signs
of connection without context,
and never anything to do with me.

When they come there's relief
But I don't hold out much hope –
too many spoiled opportunities
have made me expect less
and less, a few pleasantries,
or a chat between carers
hovering above my head.
I just long for a face
close to mine, a smile
meant just for me, a silence
I'm invited to share, a chance
to prove there's someone here.

4

Who is this man?
Where does he come from?
Where does he go to?
I've never seen him before.
He doesn't belong to me.

But he does connect with me.
He comes up and sits close
as if he's my nearest
and dearest. In a funny way
I suppose he really is.

He doesn't stay long,
but I always know he's been.
I don't look for his coming
but when he appears
I'm sure it'll be alright.

5

Who are you, and what
business do you have
pushing your face up close,
huffing and puffing and
trying to make me
open my eyes? I'll not look.
And grabbing hold of
my hand. I'll pull away.
Not today. Not today,
I'd say if I could speak.
But I'll frown and cough
and turn my head aside.
I wish he'd go. Leave me
alone. Let me get on
with my business of dying.

6

How can I tell him?
Occasionally he comes
and sits by me, holds my hand,
speaks in tones I can trust.
Sometimes he sings to me.
And the strangest thing
he does is to get up close
and match his breaths to mine.

I need him here always
but he comes and goes.

I ought to make the most
of the little he gives me,
but I don't know how.
I try to blink, smile,
move my limbs, but I can't
be sure he sees or understands.
Maybe he'll not come back.
How can I tell him?

GETTING THROUGH (2)

1

I'm a prospector of the soul,
using human tools to hand
of touching, listening, seeing
to explore the seam. The goal:
to strike gold in each being.

2

Between each intake
and each out-take
lies the mystery

Between each inhalation
and each expellation
lies the possibility.

3

Should we take the chance
of the trance and the trauma?
We really have no choice.
You're slipping away from us.
We'll hold on while we can.

And that means every device:
voice to call you up,
scents to arouse that sense,
planting a kiss Sleeping
Beauty-like on the lips.

But more often none of these –
bearing silent witness,
sharing the sounds of the day,
breathing two breaths as one,
the ground-bass of the human.

We have the moment in common.

4

All those pains welling up
that threaten to overflow

all those losses and fears
accumulations of the years

the one thing you can do
the only thing left to you

is push them out into your hands
push them out into my hands

push them out, push them away!

5

At one remove, are you secure,
safe from prying eyes and ears,
free to pursue an inner life
more real, more true, more spiritual
than anything I can aspire to?

You seem already almost through
the door that opens for us all,
but cannot tell me anything
of what lies on the other side.
Closer, yet further away?

6

Your body speaks the lines
your mouth can no longer utter
and I am here to learn them.

Each posture, every gesture,
that glint in the eye, cry, turn down
of the mouth, pressure of the fingertips –

are not to be taken in isolation,
but make up a composite
of who you were and are.

So, before it's too late, may I
be your ghost-writer? Let's create
this last chapter together.

part two

I'M HERE

I'm not bad at answering questions.
I don't try to be cheeky,
and I don't try to be smart.

This is how to go: just follow
your hand round gently
and see where it points to.
Then follow it.

I've lived here a long time.
It's not what I like best,
it's what I have to do.
Sit and be at peace,
if that's all you can do today.

You're like this: SNIP, SNIP,
SNIP, picking up every little bit
that's dropped from the lips.
Don't be leaving it around.

I very seldom put my foot in it.
And I'm not kidding.
You know where you are with me –
I'm here!

THIS PLACE

Well, I don't feel I'm at the workhouse stage yet!

My eye doesn't half bother me.
It comes out as if it's going to walk through that door.

Some people talk to you.
And some people would knock you down first.

Well, you don't know who's who and what's what here!

What do people walk like that for?
It's the way they tighten us off.

Why's she shouting at me?
It's a danger when you can't please yourself how you talk.

Well, it's better than working in the wash-house!

UP AND AWAY

Sometimes you can see where
the smoke blows right across
from the factories. Beautiful trees.
Apple blossom. It's a favourite place of mine –
wouldn't it be of yours?

Well I'll have to be off now –
temporary circumstances.

When it's stormy there
we used to nip over.
All the apples got blown off.
That's where most of them lie.
Over the terrace and over the garden.

Well I'll be on my road
or they'll be getting the guns out.

Sometimes I think about running away.
Right up through the meadow
to the cliff. It's reasonably steep.
Always keep myself trim.
There's no change in this place.

Well I'm still on a tether
so I'll have to be getting back.

A BAD 'UN

They took me leg off 18 months ago.
I've been like this ever since.
I can't even walk to the toilet.
And I hate asking them.

Her, she's got a whole leg,
and a half leg. But she can't talk.
Well, you can't have everything.

That one comes in every six months.
I don't know whether she's a Lady Mayoress
or a Sister. But it's always
"You may take my arm."

I don't like that one.
I know what he's called
but I call him 'PissQuick'.

I tell them all "You look lovely today."
Even if they've a face like a pig.

Sister calls me 'El Gobbo'.
If I swear at 'em now
I have to go to me room.
I've tried to stop it,
so I've learned to make this sign
with two fingers. It don't make
a sound but it means the same.

I've a helluva lot of friends,
but it's a long way from here to there.

I'm a bad 'un sometimes,
but I own up to it.

ROYALTY

They said I wis the Queen.
Well God A'michty help the Queen
if she's the Queen! By jings, aye,
it's terrible the jobs ye hae to dae.
To keep a smilin' face a'ways
when you feel like greetin'.
I've tried to be bright 'n cheerfu'
for the sake o' the owd folk,
because they think I'm wunnerfu'.
But I'll let ye into it:
I'm jist an ordinary wumman.

They said I wis the Queen,
'n noo when they see me
they're aye bowin 'n scrapin'
'n carryin' on as if they're nuts
– the very idea o' it!
But I dinna let on
I wis fed to the teeth wi' it,
for they made a fule o' me
when I wis forced to be naebody
'n now I'm supposed to be the Queen
they're fallen ower theirselves!

They said I wis the Queen.
'n they said I've to do sich 'n sich a thing.
'n then they stairted kneelin'
'n a' that nonsense – God,
I'm fed up to the teeth wi' it.
I'd like to get off've it.
But if ye overstep the line
ye land up in jile.
I'll let ye into it:
I'm jist an ordinary wumman
'n like folk to be chummy.

ROMANCE

I fell in love.
All on me own.
And he fell in love with me.
I didn't believe him.
He wouldn't tell me his name.
He says "I'll come and
I'll see you settled down."
And now he's sleeping with me.
But They've found out.

There's a shelf above the wardrobe
where I keep his pyjamas.
Oh, I'm alright with him,
In fact he's just my type.
The other night I put his pyjamas
in a drawer. I was asleep
when he came in. He didn't know
what to do. "Well why didn't you
climb in naked?" I asked him after.
Don't ask me where he works.
Making bodies. Car engines, you know?

First time I've slept
with anybody since
me husband died.
He makes me happy.
Not right happy, but
happy enough. Well, you know
what fellas are like, though?

ALL SINGING (1)

To me singing is most important.
When I was a child my mother sang to me.
When I saw her come into the house
I would run and jump into her lap.
In the kitchen I asked her
"Are you really singing?"
and she'd say "Yes, darling,
and it's all for you."

My father would hum to my mother,
he used to swing it, like.
He would stand with his arms around her,
and I used to love that.
He and she were very devoted.
Sometimes it seemed as if
they could draw everything to themselves.
When they used to sing it was sort of quiet,
it didn't build up to anything.
They were like Darby and Joan,
they were special, they were one.

ALL SINGING (2)

I was always singing at school,
and singing before the rest of the school.
Sometimes I'd stand in the lounge
and start singing at the top of my voice.
Perhaps the day will come when you will hear me.

I was always singing in church.
I'm not trying to be biggish, but
I can remember when my mother took me there,
to the Church, and I stood on a chair,
and everybody was clapping and shouting.

I sang all on my own quite often.
I was singing one day
and a policeman came up to me.
He asked my name.
He said "My goodness, I think you've got something."
And he gave me a lovely bunch of flowers.

Sometimes I'll sit in the house
and I'll twist it round a bit,
but nobody wants to hear my singing nowadays.

ALL SINGING (3)

A milkman came up and rang the bell once.
"Was that you singing?" he asked.
"Come on then, kiddo, let's have some more."
But I said "Sorry, I don't think there's
going to be any more as far as you're concerned."

I could try making it come through:
Life was even sweeter
than that melody.
When your lips were silent
and your eyes said you loved me.
When you played the organ
and I sang the rosary.

That song, it may be partial
but you can tell it's nice.
I like it so long as it doesn't
leave off and forget the actual.
When I'm with someone singing like this,
you know, it always fills me up.

THIS ROOM

The scenery of this room,
does it ever get changed?

Some of the compositions
are so good it would be
tragic to part with them.

Someone should photograph them
before they get changed,
or they could be lost for ever.

But at the same time
you need variety, don't you,
or you've nothing to compare?

This room should be filmed
before it is too late.

AN EYESHOT IN SUMMER

A little eyesight in the middle,
some of it retained for a purpose.

I can see a sleeve of purple.
And then there is yellow in the sky.

The trees are good and dry,
young and barking.

It's a wonderful setting,
this whole melting scene.

Is it opening or seizing?
The view – it's got the ring of expand.

CLINGING ON

How am I today?
Well, generally speaking,
standing up
in a sitting down situation.
In short, I'm ok.
Nobody's kicking
my behind. Of course,
if it's too hard
then it's a matter
for the police,
and if it's only
tickle-wickle
then it's alright.

I thought quite a lot of things
would have gone by now.
But they haven't,
they cling on.
I go out and make do,
but it's difficult to make do.

HIT OR MISS

I was dumbfounded when he said
"Mr Zed, you're finished.
Get shut o' those tools.
Dae away wi' 'em."

I was staggered when he said
"Mr Zed, you're buggered.
You're to be fitted for a pacemaker."
It came very hard.

I was amazed when he said
"Is he dead, Mrs Zed?"
when they put the wires round my head
and sent me through the chamber.

I was scared when he said
"Are you Mr Zed?
I want to put the electrics on you."
It made my body gang altogether.

I'm starting to disfigure myself
through being out of sorts.
And the worst of all my troubles?
"It's hit or miss," he said.

A LIFE IN TRADE

When I get started in my pride and joy,
it was my life, wholesale and retail.

I've been in it 30 years, in the Markets.
I'll bring you some fruit and veg.

It's hard work handling heavy goods,
make a box up, have a wrestle with it.

You automatically price your stuff.
I'm still involved a bit, but not a lot.

If I see anything that suits me now
I just have a little business deal.

You'll hear my name wherever you go,
wherever they're unloading.

PARAGLIDING AT EIGHTY

There were three of us
in the boat, and I was the first
to do it. It was the flying,
it was the feeling free.
And when I flowed like that
I was astonished. And then
I flew again: ONE, TWO, THREE!
When are we going again?

FATHER

He was well-known with one lot
and not much with the other.
I don't know where he is just now.
He was ashore, he wasn't
boats or anything just now.
I just don't know,
and we don't press too much.

I keep out of the road
because if he's annoyed
he can be awful short,
and it's himself
that annoys himself –
that takes a bit of doing!
But I'm always ready
with a cup of coffee for him,
or a cup of tea for him.
Better than rowing, isn't it?

SONG ABOUT MY FATHER

My father is right,
but not my mother.
They both hate me
and they won't help me.

He tells me when I can go out.
He tells me when I can't go out.
He punishes me for going out.

That's nothing for me,
and nothing for anybody else,
and he's shouting, shouting, shouting.

He's wanting the punch-line.
He's wanting the punch-line behind the door.
He doesn't know how much his weight is.

I can't find my father.
I can't find my mother.
I can't hate my father.
I can't hurt my father.

I'm too old for this.
I'm too old now.
I'm too old, too old,
for this responsibility.

SEEING MY SISTER

I want to go down and see my sister.
She always comes. She may come later,
but I want to see her now. I want
to see my girl, my sister.
I'm lonely – what else can I be?

If my sister came this afternoon
or in the morning, I'd know.
That would cut the day in half.
I wouldn't mind putting the one half
with the other half and sharing it out.

I wait, but she hasn't come yet.
What a person does, he's promised,
and that promise never comes,
it's discontinued, then it's gone.
And he's frustrated. It plays on his nerves.

I'm shooting myself, shooting myself –
that's what's going to happen in the end.
I can't stick it, see.
Perhaps it will get the better of me.
What'll happen is: she won't come at all in the end.

OUT OF SORTS

I don't know how long I've been here,
but it seems a long time.
Where am I? I don't know.
But I've found out more
about the people here
than they know about themselves.

There was a young man once
and he was kind and gentle.
He always spoke to me,
just for a few words,
but I was a married lady
and I lost him in the crowd.

I don't know where I am here,
I'm out of sorts. I used to be
lovely, I would speak to anybody.
Now they've got me in a pickle,
I'm a crosspatch, somebody's gone
and put a spoke in my wheel.

LOOKING UP

Why cry
when you can laugh?
It doesn't cost you anything.
You can do it all your life.
You can put it in a wee envelope in your baggage.
Or put it up on the wall
so that everyone can see it.

People think that you
need something beautiful
to make a beautiful picture.
But what you need is skill.
And the eye to see
that it is beautiful.

There's beauty in everything
if you look for it:
the sky through the skylight,
in colours or not.
It depends on your mood.

Oh I went to look up in the sky
and saw it shining there
and said, "That is Life."
Are you going to take me
to see the sun?

YOU SEE?

I'll tell you something about myself:

when I'm having a conversation
with someone like yourself,
whenever I say "I see"
I do not see,
because when I see
I don't say that but make
a sensible observation,
but when I don't quite follow
I say "I see".

That's the conclusion I've come to anyhow.

MAIR NAE ONIEBODY

I'm nae name nor nom-de-plume.
I'm naebody at a' in this hame frae hame.
I'm naebody at a' wi' trolleys inside ma daily premises.
I'm nae a tv box oniewhaur, not the one in the Smoking
    Room, an' knaw naebody in a programme.
But I wis born into this world o' sin an' frivolity.

I'm nae kleptomaniac frae Kildrummy Castle.
I'm nae a mannequin nor a fashion model an' I don't like
    new apparel.
I'm nae a cover nor a counterpane nor material for the
    thing I rest my body upon.
I'm nae a stiff apron.
But I do have a pair o' slippers on, they're Stead an'
    Simpsons, an' they fit me like a glove.

I'm nae Wordsworth, his book o' poetrie upon a
    wooden table.
I'm nae a pen, writing papers or envelopes, nor a postcard.
I'm nae an editor oniewhaur.
But I am 89 years old an' decrepit
an' I niver said onie o' this to you.

THE SLITHERER

If I were an artist
I would make a big snake-like thing,
slithering about like that,
getting away back down
into the depths, right down
into the bottom, and there
it would be.

And it's got
plenty of time, so it waits
and it waits and it waits.
Till there comes a time
when this sonofabitch
creeps up on me and says,
"I'll stiffen you, pal."
And then it's away again.

– IAN MCQUEEN

CHOOSING

Choosing? That's another thing.
Sometimes I don't know what I'm choosing.
You've got to keep hold of it,
and hopefully try and get
as much out of the first bit
that you've taken, knowing
that on the other side
the other stream will come
and knock that one out.

It's like the Snooker guys:
CLICK... TICK... CHINK...
all that sort of stuff.
it bounces off and all
the balls go into the pockets.
Or he makes wonderful hits –
down there, over there, and down there
PLINK – better than anybody else.

– IAN MCQUEEN

TAKING CARE OF THE HALO

In there, this old boy's saying
"this is ok" or mebbe
"we'll need to pull this back
a wee bit". It's like:
throw the rope out
and pull it in,
throw the rope out
and pull it in.
And you're doing that
all the time,
the brain's doing that
all the time.

It seems to be
just patterns that come,
do whatever they're doing,
disappear, and then
they probably come right round
the back and do it again.
Because my attitude is:
there's just like a halo or something
like that round there,
and it has to be there.

Because that's the kingpin,
that's the bit that sees
up, down, over –
all these things,
and that's the thing
you really have to take care of,
otherwise you can get hurt
very badly and very quickly.

– IAN MCQUEEN

DEFENCE

Bobby was bigger than me.
And when I got it, I got
a right good whack from this bloke.
He just ladled into me,
and I couldn't stotter, I was
lying in the playground. Biff! Out.

Bobby was going to get a doing.
And I administered it.
If you steam into me: Stars.
I cloaked myself in my self
and that was good for me.
I got that from him too.

I had my dose.
And Bobby had his dose.
Big Al's bigger than me too,
but I'm not going
to lie down under his blows.
He's in there. I can still
cloak myself in my self.

– IAN MCQUEEN